Our World
TEMPERATE FORESTS

Basil Booth

Illustrated by John Yates

Titles in this series

First published in 1988 by
Wayland (Publishers) Ltd
61 Western Road, Hove
East Sussex BN3 1JD, England

© Copyright 1988 Wayland (Publishers) Ltd

Edited by Hazel Songhurst
Designed by John Yates

British Library Cataloguing in Publication Data

Booth, Basil
    Temperate forests.—(Our world)
    1. Forest ecology—Juvenile literature
    2. Biogeography—Juvenile literature
    I. Title   II. Yates, John   III. Series
    910'.09152

    ISBN 1–85210–038–9

Typeset by DP Press, Sevenoaks, Kent
Printed in Italy by G. Canale & C.S.p.A., Turin
Bound in Belgium by Casterman S.A.

Front cover, main picture Autumn woodland, Europe.
Front cover, inset Acorn woodpecker, USA.
Back cover Plitvice National Park, Yugoslavia.

Contents

What are temperate forests?

Forests are large, uncultivated and unenclosed areas of woodland. Temperate forests are found in the milder (temperate) areas of the world, between the extreme heat of the tropics and the extreme cold of the polar regions. Not all of these forests are the same in structure and climate, and so varying species of trees, plants and animals can be found in each area.

Most temperate forests are made up of a mixture of broad-leaved deciduous trees (those that lose their leaves in winter). Common examples are the oak, beech and birch. These deciduous forests are found in areas with marked seasons, with short warm summers and short cold winters. Rainfall is much the same throughout the year and trees in these conditions reach heights of about 40 to 50 m.

Epiphytes and lianas are rare, although algae, lichens and mosses are abundant on trees in areas of high humidity. Animals in these forests vary their behaviour according to the seasons, with some migrating south, or hibernating, to avoid the cold weather when food is scarce. The trees lose their leaves in the winter, which helps them survive the cold weather.

Temperate rainforests are rather different, containing more animal and plant species than the deciduous forests, but not as many as those found in the steamy heat of tropical rainforests nearer the equator. Temperate rainforests are, of course, cooler than tropical forests, having well-defined seasons where temperature and rainfall vary throughout the year. Fog can be more important

The autumn colours of a mixed deciduous forest in northern Iowa, USA, signify the withdrawal of sap from the leaves.

Above Temperate rainforests lie between the deciduous forests and the lush forests of the tropics. In a wet climate free of damaging winter frosts, leaf-fall is not a necessity and the trees remain green.

Temperate evergreen woodlands occur where summer dehydration is a constant threat.

than rainfall in these forests as a source of water. Temperate rainforests contain some of the world's largest trees, including the coast redwood of the United States and the alpine ash of Australia.

Not all temperate forest trees are deciduous. In temperate evergreen woodlands, the dominant species are low shrubs that flourish in the warm, dry summers and cool, moist winters of Mediterranean-type climates. These shrubs have needles, or smaller leaves than the trees of deciduous forests, and grow to heights of only 3 to 4 m. They include tree heath, walnut, holm and cork oak, hedgehog broom and beech. Fire is a major hazard in these woodlands in dry summers, and many plants are therefore adapted to grow again quickly after being burned. As these forests are more open than others, with fewer hiding places for animals, the creatures that live there are adapted to moving quickly to escape predators.

Where temperate forests are found

Nearly all the world's temperate forests are in the northern hemisphere, forming a broken belt between the arid deserts and hot tropical rainforests to the south, and cold boreal forests to the north. The largest areas of temperate forest are found in Europe, south-east China and the eastern United States. In the southern hemisphere only a few isolated temperate forests occur in south-east Australia, Tasmania, New Zealand, South Africa and South America. There, trees such as Tasmanian snow gum, beech and alder grow.

European temperate forests consist of isolated woodlands that are the remnants of the dense forests that once covered almost the entire region. The most common trees in these woodlands include oak, beech, chestnut, sycamore and elm. Further south, on the northern border of the Mediterranean, is a more open type of temperate woodland, now extensively modified by farming and development. In China, temperate forest occupies the south-eastern part of the country. Like many other temperate forests of the world, it has been greatly changed by centuries of intensive cultivation; in northern China deforestation is more or less complete. China is the home of the tulip tree, magnolia and azalea; beech and oak trees occur in

This map shows where the world's temperate forests are found.

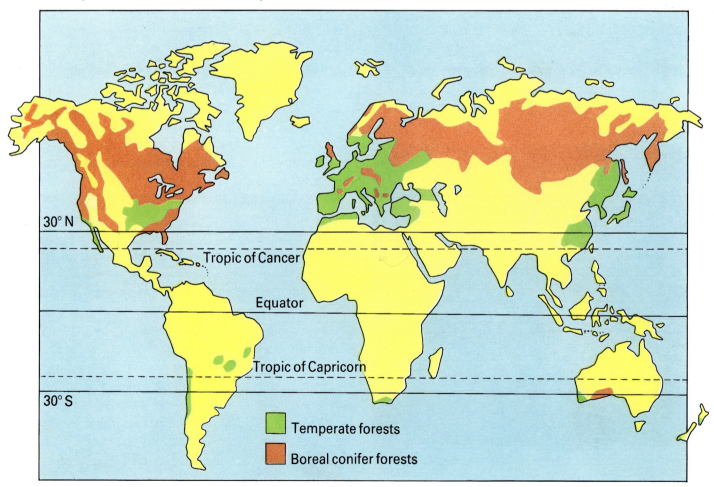

30° N

Tropic of Cancer

Equator

Tropic of Capricorn

30° S

- ■ Temperate forests
- ■ Boreal conifer forests

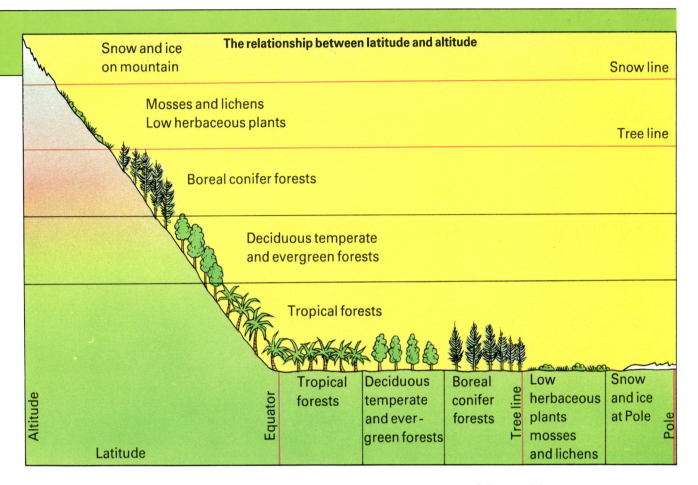

The relationship between latitude and altitude

Snow and ice on mountain — Snow line

Mosses and lichens
Low herbaceous plants — Tree line

Boreal conifer forests

Deciduous temperate and evergreen forests

Tropical forests

Altitude

Latitude

| Equator | Tropical forests | Deciduous temperate and ever-green forests | Boreal conifer forests | Tree line | Low herbaceous plants mosses and lichens | Snow and ice at Pole | Pole |

The giant redwood tree is common to the mountain forests of the western United States.

western regions of the world.

Temperate forests in the eastern United States occur mainly south of the Great Lakes and along the Appalachian mountain range, where the dawn redwood and ancient gingko (maidenhair tree) grow. Small strips of temperate woodland persist in lower California and the west coast mountains. Many European trees are found in the United States, along with maple, aspen and acacia.

Temperate trees are not just confined to temperate zones, however. With increasing altitude, climatic conditions change, temperatures are lower and seasons are more varied; this allows temperate trees to thrive on mountain ranges even in some areas of the tropics.

Ocean currents, such as the Gulf Stream, also influence climate, bringing warm conditions to cold northern coasts that would otherwise be colonized by boreal pine forests. In this way temperate deciduous woodland can be found as far north as Denmark and northern Scotland.

Development of temperate forests

Temperate forest trees had their origins about 280 million years ago, during the Permian Period, when the first conifer-like trees appeared. The gingko is the only living member of this group that once had world-wide distribution. True conifers are represented in temperate forest communities by yew, pine, larch, cedar and redwood. Spruce and other conifers occur in temperate zones, though normally they are confined to the cold boreal forests.

Most modern trees began to evolve during the Cretaceous Period, 136 million years ago, when a mild and uniform climate throughout the northern hemisphere favoured the evolution of similar floras in Europe, Asia and North America. During this period, oak, poplar, walnut and magnolia appeared for the first time. Over thousands of years, trees became adapted to their slowly changing environment through natural selection; if a tree could adapt, it survived. If not, it became extinct.

During the last Ice Age, which ended about 10,000 years ago, great ice sheets repeatedly advanced and retreated in the northern hemisphere. As the ice caps expanded in North America and eastern Asia, the plants 'migrated' south, only returning north as the ice retreated. In Europe the conditions were different, for, to the south, mountain ranges with their own ice caps formed a barrier to migration. This situation caused many species of plants to perish when the ice caps advanced. Therefore repopulation had to come from central Asia.

Pollen analysis reveals a great deal about ancient plant life and tells us that, by the end of the last Ice Age, dwarf birch and willow had become established. These were succeeded in turn by pine, elm, beech and oak, all of which were later to dominate the temperate forests of Europe and North America.

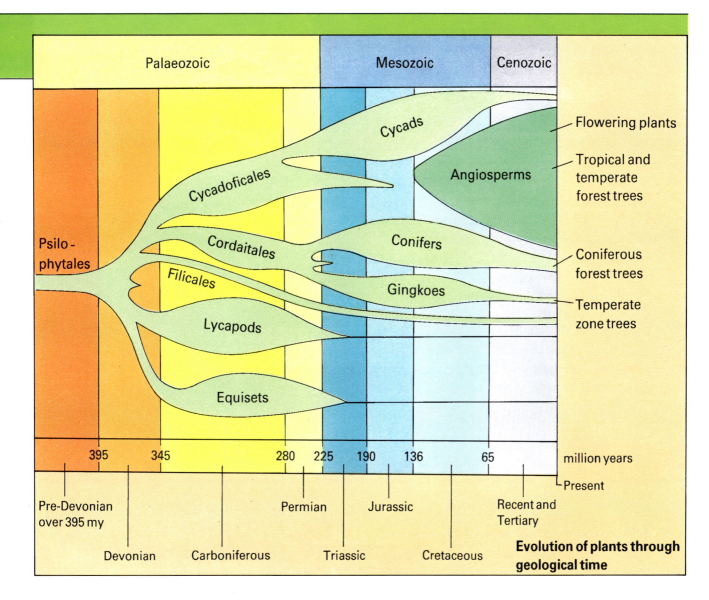

Palaeozoic					Mesozoic			Cenozoic	

Cycads

Flowering plants

Cycadoficales

Angiosperms

Tropical and temperate forest trees

Psilo-phytales

Cordaitales

Conifers

Filicales

Coniferous forest trees

Gingkoes

Temperate zone trees

Lycapods

Equisets

	395	345		280	225	190	136		65	million years

Present

Pre-Devonian over 395 my

Permian

Jurassic

Recent and Tertiary

Devonian

Carboniferous

Triassic

Cretaceous

Evolution of plants through geological time

Above Temperate trees evolved recently but conifers, cycads and gingkoes evolved over 345 million years.

Left A seedling of arctic willow, a hardy pioneer plant colonizing available space in the Greenland tundra.

Right Gingko. Its use as an ornamental tree has saved this species of an ancient group from extinction.

Plants

Plant communities are the result of ecological succession; they are organized very efficiently, and associated with complex food chains, where waste from one species is food for another.

Ecological succession begins with lichens and mosses. These are simple plants that are able to live on bare rock. Their secretions tend to break down the rock, and their remains help to create soil on which new plant species can grow. The rapid spread of tree and shrub communities, which flower and produce seed quickly, replaces these pioneer plants as soil fertility increases. The more successful communities culminate in what is called a stable climax vegetation, usually dominated by oak, beech, ash and birch, where increase in height no longer takes place.

Birch, juniper, yew and buckthorn are some of the early forerunners of temperate forest communities. Oak is a late arrival because it does not grow as quickly as other species, and its heavy acorns are not so readily dispersed as the wind-blown and bird-transported seed of other trees. However, in spite of its slow growth, oak eventually becomes established in a forest dominated by birch. Oak finally takes over as the dominant species, for birch seedlings are unable to

The needs of sea buckthorn are minimal, making it an ideal early colonizer of poor coastal soils.

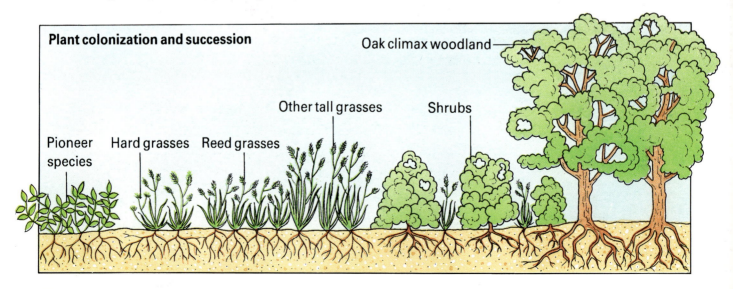

Plant colonization and succession

Oak climax woodland

Other tall grasses

Shrubs

Pioneer species

Hard grasses

Reed grasses

grow in the deep shade of the longer-lived oaks. After a century or so, birch woodland becomes oak woodland. Other community successions, where a similar process takes place, include beech to juniper woods, fenland to alder woods and ash to beech.

Each type of tree has its own ecological place. Poplars, willows and alders favour wet areas; pine prefers sandy soil; ash, yew and box like chalk or limestone; beech and oak will survive on slightly acid soils, although oak grows better on deep clays.

Where sufficient light is available, several layers of vegetation develop beneath the tree canopy. Young trees and shrubs such as yew, holly and hawthorn may support climbing plants, such as honeysuckle and ivy. Spring-flowering plants such as snowdrops and bluebells grow on the forest floor, while mosses, lichens and fungi carpet the shady, damp areas of ground.

Honeysuckle is one of a number of climbing plants that are able to use trees and bushes as support.

Below Mature deciduous forest, dominated by oak, birch and pine.

Animals

Most temperate forest animals are small, with the exception of bison, bear, deer and wild boar. The survival of the smaller creatures depends on specialization and adaptation to their environment, often to such an extent that some species depend upon one type of forest or tree, or even a particular part of that tree, such as the koala of eastern Australian forests. Most mammals live on the forest floor, although some, such as bears, racoons, chipmunks and cats, have strong, sharp claws that enable them to climb when necessary.

At ground level, racoons, badgers, small rodents, deer and pandas live on a diet of leaves, berries and seeds. In the canopy of the forest, tits, finches and squirrels feed on fruits and seeds. These plant-eating animals (herbivores) are the prey of flesh-eating animals (carnivores), such as stoats, foxes, cats, hawks and owls. Some animals are omnivores, changing from a summer diet of meat, when small plant-eating animals are easily available, to a winter diet of plant material when such meat is scarce.

Although temperate forests provide an abundant supply of insects, many species of small birds feed at different levels in the trees to ensure they do not compete with each other. Most woodland birds are insectivorous and must either migrate during the

Above Once widespread throughout Europe, the brown bear is today restricted to small areas.

Above right The polecat is widely distributed in temperate forests containing good scrub cover.

Right The eagle owl has a wingspan of over a metre and is a silent night hunter.

Left The blackbird frequents dense hedgerows and woodlands in which it can safely build its nest a few feet off the ground.

winter, when insects are scarce, or else become omnivorous and resort to eating berries and seeds. Woodpeckers and tree creepers have the advantage in winter of being able to find insects under the bark of trees. Flycatchers cannot do this, and so are forced to migrate. Nuthatches feast on the winter harvest of nuts and berries.

The shrubs beneath the trees in temperate forests are also important to small birds. Finches, tits and thrushes find shelter, perches and nesting sites there. Woodpeckers and owls like to nest inside hollow trees, while rooks, crows and hawks build their nests in the high branches of the leafy forest canopy. Birds, such as pheasants and woodcock, nest at ground level; the woodcock often nesting directly over a nest of woodmice to gain extra warmth for the incubating eggs.

Insects and other creatures

Animals without internal skeletons are called invertebrates. They vary in size from tiny organisms that can be seen only through a microscope, to large beetles and butterflies. Most invertebrates live in the forest topsoil, where their numbers may be so great that a handful of woodland soil may contain 700 million organisms. Since these minute creatures are surrounded by food they are able to grow quickly and reproduce in great numbers. A single queen wasp, for example, can produce over 12,000 offspring in one year, while millions of wood ants leave their nest on the day of their mating flight. These creatures play a vital role in the breakdown of forest waste materials, while also providing abundant food for other woodland life.

The forest is continually under attack by invertebrates. Leaves and shoots are the main food source of caterpillars. Some leaf-rolling caterpillars can defoliate mature oak woodlands, while others bore tunnels inside leaves as they feed. The lumpy swellings that sometimes grow on ash and oak are caused by gall wasp larvae. Wood-boring beetles attack oak, poplar, elm and willow, laying their eggs below the bark in small chambers. When the eggs hatch the larvae eat away side passages; when they become beetles they gnaw through the bark to the surface. Dutch elm disease is a fungus carried by such beetles; the branched side-passages down which they have gnawed can be seen on bark stripped from dead elms.

Flying insects form not only the prey of birds, but also of spiders, whose webs hang from every available bush and tree. Wolf spiders wander about the forest floor in search of prey; others hide in silken tubes from which they dart out to attack their victims.

Low-lying vegetation is attacked by slugs, snails, caterpillars and other insects, to create a continual rain of uneaten plant material, excreta and dead skin on to the forest floor; this provides nourishment for the thousands of ground-dwelling invertebrates. The breakdown of most of the forest waste takes place at this level, as ants cut up twigs, and insects such as millipedes, centipedes and beetles consume the debris.

Centipedes live in the soil and leaf litter layer, where they eat vegetation and animal refuse.

Snails are mainly nocturnal feeders, but will forage in daylight in very damp conditions.

The insects associated with a temperate forest tree.

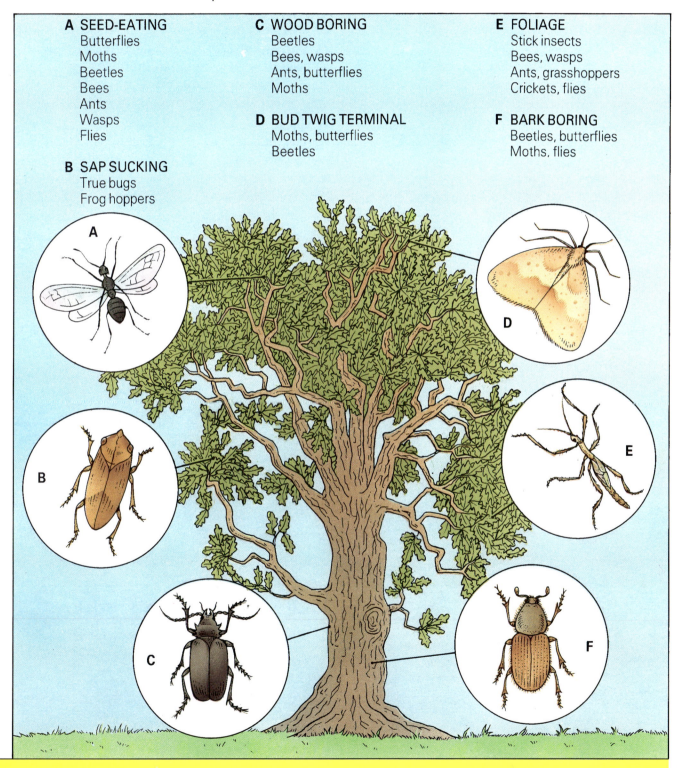

A SEED-EATING
Butterflies
Moths
Beetles
Bees
Ants
Wasps
Flies

B SAP SUCKING
True bugs
Frog hoppers

C WOOD BORING
Beetles
Bees, wasps
Ants, butterflies
Moths

D BUD TWIG TERMINAL
Moths, butterflies
Beetles

E FOLIAGE
Stick insects
Bees, wasps
Ants, grasshoppers
Crickets, flies

F BARK BORING
Beetles, butterflies
Moths, flies

The food chain

Living organisms in temperate forests rely upon each other through a complex series of events called a food chain. It is the study of these events that forms the basis of ecology.

There are five components in the food chain: autotrophs or plants (which create their own food), herbivores (plant eaters), primary carnivores and secondary carnivores (both flesh eaters) and decomposers, which break down all dead materials.

Autotrophs (plants) draw their nourishment from minerals absorbed by their roots. They also take in water and carbon dioxide which, in the presence of sunlight and green chlorophyll, is converted during photosynthesis into sugar and oxygen. Most of this oxygen is released into the atmosphere, while the sugar is available for the plant's growth during the process of respiration. On balance, more oxygen is released by plants in photosynthesis than is used in respiration.

Herbivores, which feed exclusively on plant material, include deer, squirrels, wild boar and small rodents. In summer they mostly eat foliage, but in winter, nuts, berries, bark and roots form the diet of the animals that do not hibernate or migrate.

Primary carnivores include weasels, tits, warblers, woodpeckers and beetles, for they feed on herbivores and detritivores (insects). Secondary carnivores eat primary carnivores, although many will take small herbivores as well. Wolves, foxes, wolverines, lynxes, hawks and owls are some of the most important carnivores of temperate forests.

Waste products and dead organisms provide food for the detritivores and decomposers; most of this group include invertebrates. The final breakdown of detritus is accomplished by fungi and bacteria which provide nutrients for the primary producers.

Normally the food chain is stable, but a sudden increase in one species, such as deer, can use up all of that species' available food. Some then starve, or fall prey to carnivores, and the balance is restored.

a	Aphids, leafhoppers, moths, butterflies	**i**	Fly larvae, mites, woodlice	**o**	Organic matter, dead creatures, faeces, urine
b	Spiders, stick insects	**j**	Litter humus	**p**	Fox, badger, frogs
c	**Birds feeding in canopy** Tits, warblers, parakeets	**k**	Chafer larvae, wireworms, grubs, weevil larvae	**q**	Snails, slugs, leeches
d	Caterpillars, beetles	**l**	Hawks, owls	**r**	**Large cats** Lynx
e	Woodpeckers	**m**	**Ground feeding birds** Thrush, blackbird, pigeon, woodcock	**s**	Mice, opossums
f	Woodboring grubs			**t**	Squirrels
g	Large spiders	**n**	Beetles, small spiders, beetle larvae		
h	Woodlice, spiders				

Food web of a deciduous woodland tree.

 Night activity

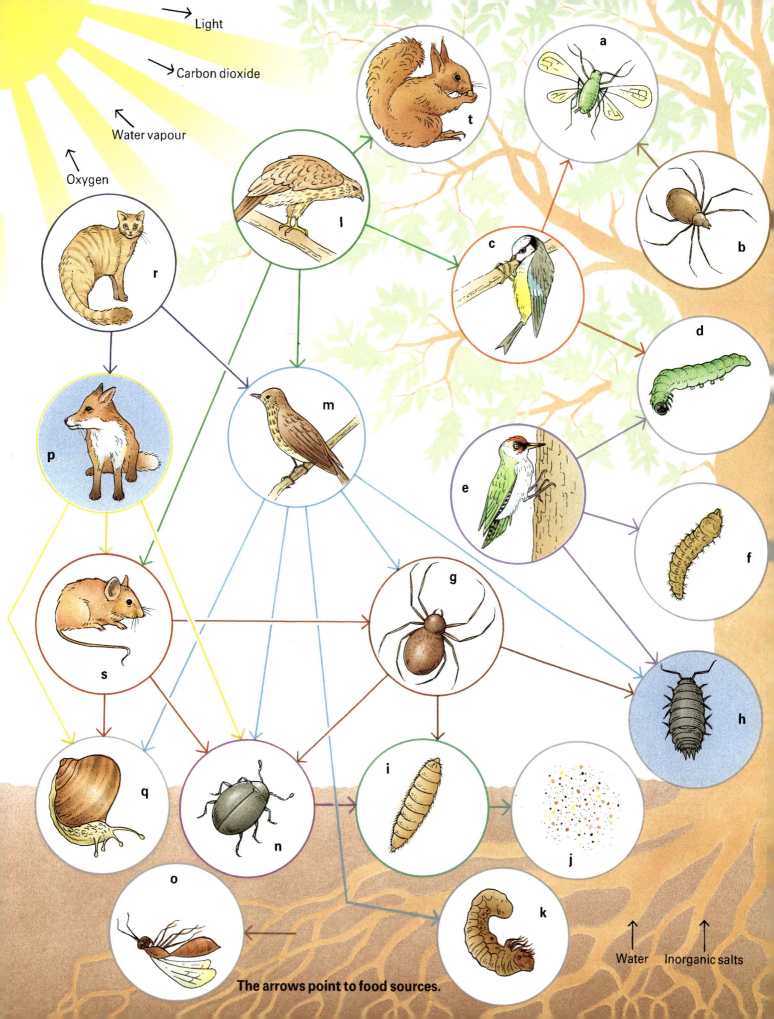

Light

Carbon dioxide

Water vapour

Oxygen

The arrows point to food sources.

Water   Inorganic salts

Spring and summer

The first indication of spring in temperate forests is the development of catkins on trees such as alder and hazel, which rely on wind blowing through the leafless branches to carry pollen to the female flowers. Before the forest's leafy canopy develops and blocks out the light, herbaceous plants such as wood anemone, dog's mercury, wood sorrel, snowdrops and bluebells must complete their flowering cycle.

As tree buds open, birds of European woodland are returning from their winter migration to Africa and southern Europe. Rooks, crows and herons rebuild last year's nests and begin to lay their eggs. Courtship displays and territorial rights are proclaimed by woodland birds, who must rule large areas to find enough food for their families. Insects then emerge and reproduce rapidly, so that the forest is soon filled with millions of caterpillars, grubs and larvae, which provide food for the increasing bird population. Foxes, badgers, hedgehogs and deer give birth to their young, while the last spring flowers carpet the forest floor and fern fronds appear through the warming damp soil.

Time is limited before the cold weather returns and this puts great emphasis on new growth. Plants must flower and produce seeds, and animals must raise their families before autumn arrives.

When the canopy deepens from the delicate green of spring, and the song of the nightingale is heard, it is a signal that summer has arrived. Herbaceous plants that can tolerate the ever-deepening shade of the forest floor burst into flower. In Europe, orchids blossom and ramsons (wild garlic) carpet the ground with their white, garlic-scented flowers. Early spring flowers have already dispersed their seed, which now begins to germinate and join other plants in the race towards available light. Some animals, having raised one family, begin on a second brood, leaving their weak, young and inexperienced offspring to fall easy prey to foxes, owls and hawks, for these predators too have families to feed. Trees continually produce new leaves, replacing those eaten by numerous generations of insects.

Above right These early wood anemones are well on the way to completing their flowering and fertilization cycle before the tree canopy develops and casts a shadow over them.

Right This family of young chaffinches is almost fledged and ready to fly. They will soon join the ever increasing number of young animals produced each spring. Many of them will fall prey to disease or to predators such as the lynx and polecat.

Left A slight movement of these hazel catkins releases clouds of pollen grains, to be captured by high-speed camera flash.

Autumn and winter

As autumn approaches the days shorten and the temperature becomes colder. Birds shed their summer plumage and develop their colourful winter feathers, ready for their courtship displays, while animal fur thickens to protect them from the approaching winter.

Trees undergo dramatic changes. In the leaves, chlorophyll is broken down and withdrawn into the tree to form energy reserves, the pigments that remain giving the tree its brilliant autumn colours. Other changes take place at the base of leaf stalks, which break off at self-healing scars. The continual rain of dead leaves to the forest floor provides new food for the decomposers. The first flushes of colourful fungi appear, shedding millions of spores from their delicate gills and pores.

As the climate cools further, mammals such as hedgehogs and badgers begin to hibernate underground, in their thick nests of leaves and grass. It is during this time that their heartbeat begins to fall to a low winter rate to conserve precious energy reserves.

The carpet of newly-fallen leaves is rich with forest produce, such as rotting fruits, seeds and nuts which, if not consumed by animals, may survive to provide new growth the following spring. Oaks and chestnuts shed thousands of acorns and nuts, but only those collected by squirrels or other rodents and buried in forest clearings will grow. Acorns cannot grow in the deep shade of the parent tree. The survival of the oak depends on animals transporting seed, just as much as the survival of these animals depends on the oak as a source of food.

As autumn merges into winter, the early morning mists are replaced by frosts. Only the hardy plants retain their leaves, providing animals with shelter from the biting winds, rain and snow. Days are at their shortest now and it is time for forest wildlife to search for food, for when the ground is deep with snow only the hardy and resourceful survive. The snow, however, brings an advantage, protecting delicate plants from the frosts that would otherwise kill them.

Left The vivid colours on this maple tree signify the onset of autumn, as sap is withdrawn and complex chemicals break down, leaving pigments behind.

Right Locked in the grip of white snow, life in the Black Forest of West Germany drops almost to a standstill. Only hardy carnivores emerge in search of food, whilst the remaining fauna slumber on in their hiberation burrows.

Early settlements

Several thousand years before man settled in Europe, great natural forests of oak, beech, ash, lime, elm, alder, hazel and pine covered the landscape in an almost endless range. Around 7500 BC, early man was becoming adapted to life in the mixed oak forests that had developed since the last Ice Age. At first, Stone Age man is believed to have survived on woodland produce such as fruit, berries and nuts, but soon learned to hunt forest animals that had existed previously on open tundra.

By 4500 BC, Stone Age man had migrated over much of Europe, and possibly North America, and had discovered the value of wood for making weapons and shelters. It was in Neolithic times, around 2400 BC, that more intensive settlement of the forests began. Trees were felled to make way for fields of wheat and barley, the cut timber being used for fuel and building. Wild animals were domesticated by man; pigs, sheep, goats and cattle were raised in enclosures to provide a year-round

Early villages were enclosed in a strong wood stockade. Thatched roof stays were often set into the ground enclosing a simple timber house.

Left Two Celt villagers forging tools and weapons from iron heated in a primitive wood-fired furnace.

supply of food. Bee keeping, initiated by the Persians, provided honey, as well as wax for making candles.

It was the Celts (700 BC onwards) who first realized the value of iron. They manufactured weapons and tools that were far superior to earlier designs. With their new sharp axes they were able to fell trees more easily and build more homes, burial chambers and boats; that timber which could not be used for building provided fuel for heating, iron smelting and pottery firing. The timber homes gradually became more elaborate, offering increased protection against the elements. The extra warmth they provided during severe winters resulted in fewer deaths for man and his livestock and was partly responsible for the successful increase in the population. Settlement clearings continued to grow at the expense of the forest, more houses were built and more land put under the plough to feed an ever-increasing community.

By carefully exploiting forest resources, self-sufficient village communities developed. Roads were cut through forests to link settlements that were able to trade with each other; the larger ones becoming centres for regular sales of livestock, often accompanied by celebrations and, later, fairs. Many of these settlements survived to become the towns and villages of today.

Agriculture

As man established plots of cultivated land in the forests, the gathering of woodland produce no longer became a necessity. This new agricultural land was created by cutting and burning trees and undergrowth, the ash from the fires providing a fertilizer for the crops that were to be planted.

It was between AD 1000 and 1200 that agriculture developed rapidly in Europe, creating a new wealth in the wake of the vanishing forests that were felled to make way for villages, towns, farmland and roads. The rapid spread of agriculture was the result of an expanding population, much of which migrated to eastern Europe, the Mediterranean and the Holy Land. By AD 1200 the newly-won soil was being ploughed by teams of oxen and planted with crops of spring oats and barley, and autumn wheat and rye. These were harvested and ground between stones to provide flour for making bread.

Land usage passed through the three-field

With his sharp iron tools man was able to fell trees more easily and build stronger homes.

Established cultivated plots around a medieval manor

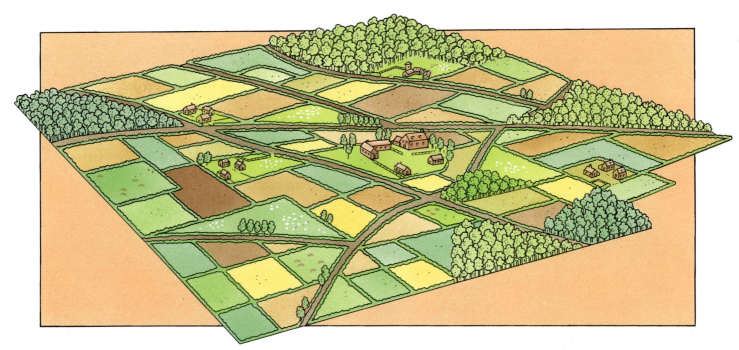

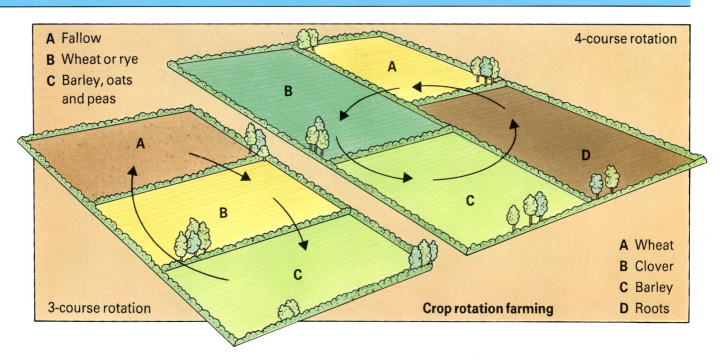

A Fallow
B Wheat or rye
C Barley, oats and peas

4-course rotation

A Wheat
B Clover
C Barley
D Roots

3-course rotation

Crop rotation farming

rotation system of the Middle Ages (where the succession was fallow, then wheat or rye, then barley or pulses) to a four-field system in the eighteenth century. Here, the succession was wheat, clover, barley, rootcrops; this eliminated the fallow year and increased productivity.

Fruits have always been an important part of man's diet and the importing of rose and citrus family trees that could be grown in temperate forest zones, such as apples, pears, oranges and lemons, gave increased variety. Plums, sloes, raspberries and blackberries were common in many ancient forests and were cultivated in the early clearings to yield produce that could be eaten fresh or dried for future use.

Temperate forests in North America suffered a similar fate to those in Europe, the main difference there being that agricultural practices had evolved considerably by the time the first European settlers cut forest clearings to build their homesteads and begin farming. Cereals, pulses and rootcrops, that also formed the basic diet of the forest-dwelling Native Americans, were supplemented by poultry and other livestock imported by the settlers.

Above The 3-course rotation system of farming was later succeeded by the 4-course system.

Below Cattle rest in the shade of an isolated tree, left for this purpose when a temperate forest was destroyed to make way for agricultural land

Exploration

Forests have always been a barrier to travel, and created difficulties for the early explorers who sought routes through them. The Phoenicians, based on the Syrian coast, were enthusiastic explorers. During the twelfth century BC they established trade routes across the Pyrenees mountains to the south of France, and through the dense forests of Germany and Austria. The Celts' economy was also based on mixed farming and trade, and they too explored and colonized the forests of central Europe, establishing numerous hill forts and expanding their empire westward into Spain, northward to Britain and east to the Black Sea.

Even the northward expansion of the powerful Roman Empire was halted by the density of the forests of Germany. Instead, their trade routes eventually became established through France, Austria, Belgium and Hungary where navigable rivers provided natural routes through the wilderness. It was on the banks of these trade route rivers that many of today's towns and cities were founded. Where navigable rivers were absent the

Above Temperate forest still covers this region of Hangzhov in China, in spite of wholesale destruction in many other areas.

Below Dense, mixed deciduous forest clothes the slopes of ridge after ridge in the Appalachian Mountains in Tennessee, USA.

forests remained unexplored for a long time. A similar situation arose after the European discovery of North America, when settlers from Europe made their homes on the east coast. Once again the forests proved a formidable obstacle to settlement, and it took American colonists nearly 200 years to reach and settle in the centre of the dense Appalachian forests.

Remoteness, terrain and hostile natives hindered early exploration of South American temperate forests, while exploration in southern Chile was made difficult by a ban on trading that was not lifted until the late eighteenth century.

Temperate forests in Australasia are generally more open than most and although rivers formed the main routes for exploration, resistance from tribesmen proved to be the main obstacle.

From the eighteenth century onwards, exploration was carried out by scientific expeditions. Botanists, from institutes like those at Kew in England and Montpellier in France, together with plant breeders, sought new and exotic species that could be cultivated in Europe and North America. Magnolias and azalias were discovered in the Himalayas and the mountains of China and later introduced into parks and gardens. Sumacs, whose leaves turn brilliant red in autumn, and eucalyptus, with its rich scent, are both able to grow in sheltered northerly temperate zones, far away from their native south-east Asia. Many of the trees in public parks owe their presence to the successes of such scientific exploration.

Salzburg, Austria. This area was once thickly forested and the River Salzach provides the only easy access route.

Timber

There are roughly 405 million hectares of temperate forest in the world. Together with coniferous wood, they supply nearly all the timber used by man. The largest supply of temperate hardwood comes from the United States, which itself uses over two-thirds of the world's timber requirements. Oak comes from Europe and Japan, and walnut from eastern Turkey and Siberia.

There are two kinds of timber: softwood from conifers, and hardwood from broadleaved forests. Tree trunks are made up of concentric layers. On the surface is the bark which protects the inside from damage by animals and the climate; beneath this is the phloem, which transports nutrients up and down the tree. Separating these from the valuable centre is the cambium, a thin layer of cells from which the outer phloem and the inner sapwood grow. Sapwood transports water from the roots to the leaves, but when the inner sapwood ceases to function it becomes filled with by-products, such as lignin, and becomes the hard, strong heartwood that is responsible for supporting the tree. Heartwood contains knots which are the thinner heartwood of branches arising from the tree core. Because of this, heartwood cannot be used for making planks. Sapwood, which has fewer knots, is used instead. Bark is broken up for cheap fuel or used as topsoil dressing, initially to reduce evaporation and later to decompose into organic nutrients.

High quality timber was extensively used in the past to manufacture furniture.

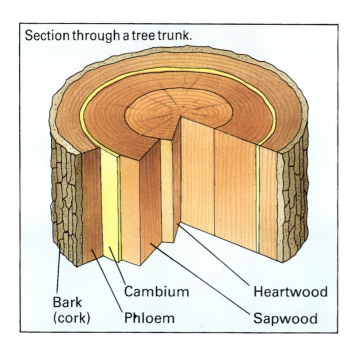

Section through a tree trunk.

Bark (cork)
Cambium
Phloem
Heartwood
Sapwood

This efficient use of trees means that there is little waste. The outer, curved planks go to make chipboard, now increasingly used in the manufacture of low-cost furniture. Some trees are shaved into thin sheets to make plywood, layers of thin wood glued together to make strong pliable boards.

Some of the best and most valued timbers from temperate forests are walnut, yew, elm, beech and oak, which are used to make high-quality furniture.

One of the reasons for the loss of Europe's forests was the insatiable demand for timber, especially by shipbuilders. For one large boat, such as was used by Spain in the Armada, 300 oaks were felled for ribs and hulls and 300 pines for decking and spars. In addition, walnut was used for rudders and elm for the capstans.

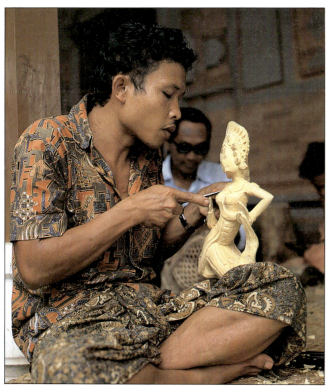

This wood carver in Bali carefully fashions the figure of a dancer from local timber.

Above Pine logs lie cut and ready for transporting to the timber mill.

Food

One of the earliest fruits grown by man was the fig. It was cultivated in Syria's southerly temperate zone in 4500 BC and referred to in the Bible as a staple food. Another was the olive, which provided oil for cooking, as well as an edible fruit that could be preserved.

Apples probably originated in southern Asia. Some sweeter pippins imported into England by Henry VIII's gardener became the forerunners of today's high-sugar dessert apples and high-acid cooking apples. Cider, made from fermented apple juice, owes its flavour to the apple's various natural aromatics. Wild, or crab, apples are probably a genetic reversal of cultivated species; the original wild variety remains unknown. Most cultivated apples are the work of over 2000 professional scientific breeders, who combine the desirable characteristics by cross-pollination and perpetuate the best hybrids by grafting. In spite of this, it is the chance seedlings that have given some of the best varieties on the market today. Apples are used to make cider, for wine, liqueurs, vinegar, preserves and dried fruits. Over 22 million tonnes of apples are harvested annually.

Damsons, greengages, apricots, peaches and cherries are all members of the plum family, with over 13 million tonnes being produced annually from fruits that originated in Asia and China 2000 years ago. Most have limited keeping qualities and are therefore tinned, bottled, dried, or used to make various drinks.

Many of these soft fruits grow only in southerly

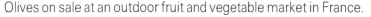
Olives on sale at an outdoor fruit and vegetable market in France.

Above Cherries are one of the many soft fruits that grow on trees.

Left Citrus fruits such as oranges and lemons are used to make refreshing soft drinks.

temperate zones. Pears originated from the hybridization of various wild species, the best-quality trees being propagated by grafting to ensure continuation of the hybrids. Today, many fruits are harvested early, whilst firm enough to withstand transportation, and are artificially ripened in special warehouses after importation.

Other foods provided by temperate forest trees include nuts from hazel, walnut, chestnut, and hickory (pecan nut trees); sugar and syrup from the maple; seeds from the stone pine, and mace from the nutmeg tree. Gin derives its aromatic flavour from the unripe berries of the juniper tree.

Products from trees

One of the earliest uses of wood was to make hunting tools such as axe shafts, bows and spears. Today, bows are still made for sport, but from Spanish cedar and not yew, as in the past. Wood still has many important uses, especially in the construction of buildings and furniture. It is also used in minor industries, including the manufacture of cricket bats and orchestral instruments such as violins and pianos.

Apart from its use as timber, wood is also used in the manufacture of paper and in the chemical industry. Although not affecting broad-leaved forests so much as coniferous forests, the paper industry uses vast numbers of trees that are otherwise unfit for use as timber. The wood is chopped, ground very fine and then pulped to be reconstituted into thin sheets of paper for use in packaging, writing paper, newspapers and books.

The chemical industry relies upon the careful distillation of wood, mainly from coniferous trees such as pine, to produce turpentine for the paint industry, and essential oils and alcohol for cosmetics and fuel. The residues from distillation are pitch, tar, resins and waxes. Their uses range from caulking boat seams to the manufacture of furniture polish. Other chemical products include gums and dyes, acetic acid and vitamins, oils and fats and alkaloids and tannins. Their uses range from medicine and food preservation to leather tanning.

Firewood and charcoal account for half of the world's cut trees, with over 80 per cent being used as fuel in developing countries. Charcoal is made from wood burned in low-oxygen conditions.

Some minor products involve the use of special trees, such as osiers for basket-work and hazel for fencing and thatching.

Another use of trees is as living ornaments in our parks and gardens. Many trees are imported for this purpose, one of the few uses that does not involve their destruction.

Above Charcoal burning in Indonesia provides smokeless fuel.

Sheets of cork stripped from a cork oak in Portugal lie stacked for drying.

Right Piles of firewood provided by woodland management, when weak or unwanted trees are removed from a forest.

Conservation and leisure

Hiking is a popular pastime in Yellowstone National Park, USA.

In ancient times the Greeks looked upon trees with great respect. They associated them with gods: oak with Zeus, olive with Athena and laurel with Apollo. When forests were felled, the Greeks left individual trees, or clumps, as holy relics. Unfortunately, trees have not always received such reverent treatment.

In medieval times in Europe exploitation of natural forests was in the hands of the sovereign, who often donated land to loyal barons. It was between the fifteenth and nineteenth centuries that naval powers not only exploited forests to provide timber for shipbuilding, but also supplemented them by importing and planting many new species. Landscape gardening and arboreta (botanical gardens specializing in trees) became fashionable in the eighteenth century, when landscape architects such as 'Capability' Brown established artificial landscapes and tree collections in the grounds of wealthy estates.

After the Second World War, large areas of Europe needed rebuilding, and some towns and cities were redesigned to include more trees, parks and landscaped gardens. The countryside came under scrutiny and select areas, which included natural woodlands, were given special protection against urban development. Today we are aware of the vital part trees play in ecology, and attempts are being made to protect our environment. Tree conservation has come of age.

Many motorways are now shielded by specially-planted trees from winds and drifting snow, creating less monotonous scenery, increasing road safety and reducing traffic noise. In 1986, hedgerows were being replanted to replace those torn out earlier by farmers. Hedgerows have been the home of many trees and animals since very early times.

Urban forestry is the name given to the management of woodlands to provide amenities and recreational facilities for people who live in

nearby towns and cities. The idea, first developed in the northern pine forests of Canada, is now applied to many forests in the western world. Such woodlands are managed by forestry commissions, local authorities or trusts for nature conservation. Many of these woodlands also form part of a valuable economic industry, the trees being felled as they mature and the ground replanted with saplings. Commercial forests, too, can play their part in recreation: in North America and Europe much of this forested land has been made accessible to the public, and study centres and marked nature trails have been set up to encourage a greater understanding of our environment.

Left A natural history photographer patiently waits to photograph a bird.

Below Fly fishing for trout in mountain streams is a popular recreation in many countries.

National Parks

National Parks are areas of natural beauty set aside by governments especially for the enjoyment of visitors and the protection of animals and plants.

Yellowstone Park, in the United States, was the world's first National Park, created in 1871 after the exploration of the area by the United States Geological Survey. At first, policing was carried out by the army, but in 1916 the National Park Service was formed with its own organized staff of rangers.

Europe followed the lead given by the USA and established the Swiss National Park in the Alps. Consisting of 169 sq km of forest and grassland, the park thrives on a policy of 'non-intervention'. Firs, beech, elm, oak and lime make up much of the woodland, while ibex, chamois, golden eagle and eagle owl are part of the park's rich fauna. Other bird inhabitants include capercaillie, snow finch and ring ouzel. Each year more than 300,000 people visit the beautiful valleys and mountains.

In northern Italy, the Stelvio National Park is by far the largest in Europe, covering over 1,370 sq km adjacent to the Swiss National Park. Stelvio's amenities include hotels, tourist huts, ski lifts and good road access. The largest forest in Europe, however, is the Bayerischerwald in West Germany. Here, an area of 130 sq km of mixed woodland, dominated by beech, spruce and silver fir, has almost reverted to its natural state. The honey buzzard, Ural owl, and red-breasted flycatcher are part of its rich bird life. To encourage visitors there is a 37-hectare play woodland for children, nature trails and several amenity centres which are designed to attract tourists away from sensitive parts of the forest, where the pressure of too many visitors could be damaging.

The most profitable of all National Parks, however, is the Plitvice Lakes Park in northern Yugoslavia, where 1300 people are employed in hotels, restaurants and commercial developments related to tourism. This park caters for nearly one million tourists each year and is famous for its sixteen lakes linked by waterfalls. It also contains virgin forests of beech, fir and spruce, where, to protect the trees, no visitors are allowed.

Home of the legendary Robin Hood, Sherwood Forest in Britain is a well-organized recreation centre. The centre has special educational facilities for children, shops, and exhibitions on conservation.

Tourists cross one of the many spectacular lakes in Yugoslavia's Plitvice National Park.

Early morning is the best time to see animals, such as this moose in Yellowstone National Park, before the hundreds of visitors force them to the seclusion of the forested hills.

New land for farming

As demand has increased for food to feed a rapidly expanding world population, so the rich soil of the temperate forests has been steadily used up by modern agriculture. The original prehistoric 80 per cent forest cover in the USA has now fallen to 30 per cent. On average, only 15 per cent remains in Europe, varying from 3 per cent in Ireland to 26 per cent in Germany. Britain's original 80 per cent tree cover is now reduced to 6 per cent. Not all of this depletion is due to land being turned over to farming; the growth of urban centres, use by industry and mismanagement of resources must all share the blame.

Trees are vital to our ecology. They influence climate, returning up to 75 per cent of rainfall to the atmosphere by evaporation and transpiration through their leaves. When forests are cut down to provide new land for farming, this process ceases and the water returned to the atmosphere falls to under 25 per cent. The remaining 75 per cent runs off the surface of the land, putting pressure on drainage systems and washing away soil, causing erosion during wet seasons. The wet seasons then gradually become fewer as the atmosphere is starved of water vapour and, as a result, droughts become increasingly frequent. Such misuse of newly created farming land led to the dustbowl conditions of the 1930s in parts of the Midwest of the United States, where 1m of soil was removed by wind erosion. Today, millions of tonnes of soil are

Only temperate forest trees that cling to steep hills and cliffs in the Ober Danau National Park, West Germany, are safe from the advance of agriculture.

Above Here, in western Australia, extensive soil erosion and gullying has followed clearance of gum forests for agricultural use.

Below An overflowing grain store in Europe.

lost there annually. Even in East Anglia, a flat area of eastern England, dust storms have occurred following similar land clearance schemes. Fertile and fairly flat land is needed if food is to be grown successfully on a commercial scale, and not all natural forests provided such conditions. Those that did have now been felled, ploughed and planted.

Adequate rainfall, temperature and day length are very important in agriculture, and influence the type of crops that can be grown. However, with advances in the breeding of plants, new varieties are constantly being produced to give maximum crop output under the limits imposed by nature. The result is overproduction of many food crops in the western world and the growing mountains of grain in western Europe.

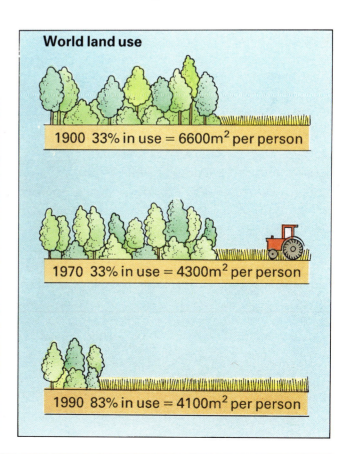

World land use

1900 33% in use = 6600m² per person

1970 33% in use = 4300m² per person

1990 83% in use = 4100m² per person

Pollution and disease

When the Industrial Revolution began in Europe and North America during the eighteenth century, little thought was given to the long-term effects of pollution. Today the problem is acute, with large areas of forest in Europe and parts of North America dying as a result of acid rain falling from an increasingly polluted atmosphere. Pollution is a global problem, but is particularly severe in developed countries, which are responsible for releasing thousands of tonnes of chemicals and dust into the atmosphere annually. The main sources of pollution are exhaust from jet planes, cars and trucks, fumes from domestic heating, forest fires and, worst of all, waste matter from factories. The contaminants include carbon monoxide, solid particles, hydrocarbons, nitrogen oxides and sulphur dioxide. Sulphur dioxide is oxidized in the atmosphere to form sulphur trioxide; this combines with water to produce sulphuric acid, a corrosive substance which eventually falls as rain — sometimes long distances away — where it defoliates and kills trees.

Disease also takes its toll of our trees, causing enormous financial losses in commercial forests. Many diseases are due to very specific fungal growths that infect only one type of tree. Apple scab, for example, is a fungus that attacks the leaves and fruit of apple trees, causing scabby disfiguration and making the fruit unsaleable. Chestnut blight is another fungal disease that has destroyed large numbers of trees in North America. Dutch elm disease has devastated the elm population in Europe. Trees are most susceptible to attack by disease when they are weakened by drought, soil pollution or waterlogging. These disease-causing organisms, however, are part of the forest's way of disposing of weak and old trees, for they fall and rot down, providing humus and nourishment for younger specimens. Most problems of disease are the result of man's intervention in nature.

Above A coal-fired power station in England pumps out gases and smoke to pollute the atmosphere.

Above Galleries eaten away beneath elm bark by the wood-boring beetle which carries Dutch elm disease.

Right The Black Forest of Germany is particularly at risk from acid rain.

Struggle for survival

The increasing pollution of the atmosphere, waterways and land, has helped create environments alien to many forms of life. Species struggle to survive but in many cases they are unsuccessful. Man's introduction of foreign species of animals and plants, with which the native species is unable to compete, has also often been a failure, for it is not always possible to foresee the effect the introduced species might have on the environment. The grey squirrel, for example, was thoughtlessly introduced into Britain from North America, and now it is regarded as a pest. It adapted and bred quickly, feeding on the bark of beech, sycamore and oak, as well as cereal crops and young birds. As a result it was able to compete with the native red squirrel on much stronger terms and reduce it to a tiny population. Because of the needs of modern forestry, conifers have now replaced large areas of natural deciduous woodland, with the resultant loss of much of the wildlife that once lived

Above A young grey squirrel, the descendant of an American species introduced into Britain.

Below Experts guess it will take 200 years to restore Britain's trees destroyed by the 1987 hurricane.

Above A scientist in Germany measures the atmospheric contamination from a power station.

Below Reforestation programmes with rapid-growing trees are today helping to restore the forest cover.

there. Early New Zealand settlers introduced carnivores such as dogs, cats, stoats and weasels, and herbivores such as deer and pigs. Their wild descendants were responsible for the destruction of many native animals, birds and trees.

The establishment of National Parks and the work of nature conservation groups has helped stem the tide of destruction, but in spite of their increasing efforts they have to battle continually with the need of modern society for more land, and the effects of development, pollution, destruction due to mismanagement, and the overuse of forests. Because of man's widespread exploitation of temperate forests, one crop grows where once there was diversity. No responsible society can demand both unrestricted access to temperate woodlands and conservation at the same time. Action on a global scale is now needed if our forests are to be saved and restored to just a fraction of their former splendour.

Glossary

Acetic acid   The acid contained in vinegar.

Alkaloid   A chemical of plant origin that contains nitrogen.

Angiosperm   Any flowering plant.

Arid   Dry due to low seasonal rainfall.

Aromatics   Substances with a fragrant or spicy smell.

Boreal   An area of the north, between the temperate and Arctic zones.

Broad-leaved   Used to describe trees with broad rather than needle-shaped leaves.

Cambium   The layer of cells in the stems and roots of plants that produces heartwood and phloem (which transport water and nutrients up and down the outer part of the plant).

Capstan   A revolving barrel for winding ropes on sailing ships.

Caulking   The waterproof material packed between the planks of a wooden vessel to prevent leakage.

Concentric   Having a common centre (i.e. layers one inside the other).

Cordaitales   Extinct trees that had tall slender trunks and branching crowns.

Conifers   Trees that produce their seeds in cones, such as pine and spruce. Most conifers are evergreen with needle-shaped leaves.

Cycadofilicales   Extinct plants that resembled modern tree ferns.

Cycads   The small group of fern-like plants.

Deciduous   Used to describe plants that shed their leaves annually.

Defoliate   To remove leaves. Defoliation is usually caused by disease or insect attack.

Deforestation   The clearance of all woodland.

Detritus   Waste material produced by discarded material, such as leaves, dead matter, shed hairs and feathers.

Detrivores   Creatures that eat detritus.

Distillation   The process of evaporating or boiling a liquid and condensing its vapour.

Diversity   Different kinds, or species.

Ecology   The study of the relationships between living organisms and their environment.

Epiphytes   Plants that use other plants as a support but derive no nourishment from them.

Equisetes   The small group of plants that include horsetails.

Excreta   Waste expelled from the body.

Exploitation   The working of, for example, a forest, to make money (e.g. timber, agriculture).

Fallow   Land that is ploughed but left unseeded to improve its quality.

Flora   The plants of a particular area or period of time.

Fronds   The leaf-like parts of ferns, formed by the union of stem and foliage.

Gingko   A tree with unusual fan-shaped leaves that originates from China. It is also known as the maidenhair tree.

Grafting   Transplanting living material, for example, the insertion of a bud or twig into another part of a plant to give stronger growth or a better crop.

Hardwood   The wood of broad-leaved trees, such as oak, ash, beech (as distinguished from softwood which comes from conifers).

Herbaceous   Plants that do not have woody stems.

Herbivore   An animal that eats only plant material.

Humus   Decayed vegetable material.

Hybridization   Cross-breeding to produce stronger varieties.

Hybrid   A plant or animal produced by cross-breeding.

Liana   A climbing and twining plant; usually tropical.

Lignin   The substance that thickens the cell walls of plants to give them great strength.

Litter   Material used as bedding for animals.

Lycopods   The group of plants that includes clubmosses.

Middle Ages   The years between AD 1000 and AD 1500.

Navigable   A waterway which is wide, deep or safe enough to be sailed on or through.

Omnivore   An animal that eats both plant and animal material.

Osiers The cut branches of willow that are used for basketwork.

Pathogen An organism that causes disease.

Perpetuate To continue for ever.

Phloem The layer of cells outside the cambium (from which they are produced) that transports nutrients up and down a plant.

Phoenicians Ancient inhabitants of part of Syria.

Pollen analysis The study of living and fossil pollen grains and plant spores.

Propogate To multiply plants by taking cuttings.

Pulses Edible seeds such as peas, soya beans and lentils.

Rainforests Dense forests found in tropical areas of heavy rainfall. The trees are broad-leaved and evergreen.

Specialization Adaptation to a particular purpose.

Succession A number of things following one another in order.

Tannin A substance produced from bark and used for preparing leather.

Temperate A mild climate with warm wet summers and cold wet winters.

Transitional A change from one place, or condition, to another.

Transpiration The release of water vapour and gases from leaf surfaces.

Tundra The barren Arctic regions where subsoil is permanently frozen.

Further reading

Brown, W.H., *Timber* (Wayland, 1977).

Cloudsley-Thompson, J.L., *Guide to Woodlands* (British Naturalists Association/Crowood Press, 1985).

Duffey, E., *National Parks and Reserves of Western Europe* (Macdonald, 1982).

Hora, B. (ed.), *The Oxford Encyclopaedia of Trees of the World* (Peerage, 1986).

Mitchell, A., *Trees of Britain and Northern Europe* (Collins, 1984).

Mitchell Beazley Joy of Knowledge Library *Vol: The Natural World* and *Vol: The Physical Earth* (Mitchell Beazley, 1977).

Neal, E., *Woodland Ecology* (Heinemann, 1953).

Lambert, Mark, *Focus on Paper* (Wayland, 1986).

Langley, Andrew, *Focus on Timber* (Wayland, 1986).

Page, Jake, *Forest* (Time-Life Books Inc, 1984)

Rowland-Entwistle, Theodore, *Jungles and Rainforests* (Wayland, 1987).

Index

Picture acknowledgements

The publishers would like to thank the following for allowing their photographs to be reproduced in this book: Bruce Coleman Ltd front cover (main picture/Hans Reinhard; inset/B.&C. Calhoun), 5 (top/Michael Fogden), 8 (Robert Burton), 12 (top/Hans Reinhard), 32 (Alain Compost), 33 (Mark N. Boulton), 41 (Hans Reinhard), 42 (N.G. Blake). GeoScience Features Library 4, 10, 12 (bottom), 13, 14, 18, 19, 27, 36, 37, 38, 39, 40, 42, 43, back cover. The Hutchison Library 5 (bottom), 19 (bottom), 30, 34, 38, 39. Oxford Scientific Films 9 (G.I. Bernard). ZEFA 7, 13, 14, 20, 21, 28, 29, 31, 32, 35, 43. Illustration on p. 22 is by John James. Illustrations on pp 23, 24 are by Mark Bergin.